# THE MIXED URN

## Carol Rumens

## The Sheep Meadow Press

The Sheep Meadow Press
P.O. Box 84
Rhinebeck, NY 12514

Designed and typeset by Sheep Meadow Press
Distributed by Syracuse University Press

Library of Congress Cataloging-in-Publication Data


Names: Rumens, Carol, author. 1944.
Title: The mixed urn / Carol Rumens
Description: Rhinebeck, NY : Sheep Meadow Press, [2019]
Identifiers: LCCN 2019028313 | 978-1-937679-87-3 (pbk.)
Classification: LCC PR6068.U6 A6 2019 | DDC 821/ .914--dc23
LC record available at: https://lccn.loc.gov/2019028313

Acknowledgements to the editors of the following journals:
*About Larkin, Agenda, Fortnightly Review, New Welsh Review,*
*The Manhattan Review, PN Review, Strix, the TLS.*

Thank you to Gomer Press, for permission to reproduce material
from *A Wider Sky* by Kyffin Williams.

*"Swept Beyond Penmon: Kyffin Williams and the After-Sea"*
draws on an interview for the British Library with the artist
by Cathy Courtney.

*"The Hazel Nut"* was commissioned by Michael Chant
of the Cornelius Cardew Trust for the themed concert,
*"One World,"* performed at Morley College, London, 18.01.2019.

An early draft of *"Freedom's Twilight"* was published
in *Perhaps Bag*, Sheep Meadow Press. 2017.

Thanks to Professor Greg Nagy, to Matina Goga, and to all
at the Harvard Center for Hellenic Studies, Nafplio, Greece,
where my Michael Marks award residency in March, 2019 was based.

Special thanks to Stanley Moss, great poet, and
sterling shepherd of the flock at Sheep Meadow.

# CONTENTS

# THE MIXED URN

## The Mixed Urn

Storm-addict Zeus, we're told
on good authority, maintains two urns
for forcing human fate,
He flings handfuls from one, then the other –
a slug of grief, and now some tinkling gold.
If there's any third, a mixed urn —
it's us, poor contradictions,
thrown together, trying to go straight
on two unlikely feet.
If only we'd been filled
with just the luck required to hunt and gather
and eat and fuck, we wouldn't have needed Zeus —
our boss, our lord, our loony lightning-rider.

There'd be no gods with urns under their beds.
Nor Homer, either.

## A Tale for the President

Before you were born, there was this *malchik*; look,
he's six today, with his class of six-year-olds singing
*Let there ALways be SUNshine,*

He wins the war with a gameplan of beetroot raids.
Sputnik in space, iron fins in the bay, Papa's
Samurai sword will dance with the Elvis demon…

Look, the *malchik* twists into the waves,
the women his waves, America his wavelength,
the *detski saad* still singing.

He marches under the spun-gold spire, this *malchik* —
*Let there ALways be BLUE sky* —
and out again. An angry, weeping father

quickly cups his hand — *the lad's gone spying* —
*hush — for our motherland!* The *malchik* sings *My bonnie
lies over the ocean…* Before you cut off his head,

wipe off the shadowy baseball cap, the tears for Stalin,
the long frontal ache… *stilled on my pillow.*
Beside Welsh birches stooped, your white-haired *malchik*

planted a sapling, *gingko biloba,*
and rustling years in thousands sighed that hope
may grow, legend by legend, till it returns,

green as bottles of spring-water. Vladimir
Vladimirovich**,** the *malchik* always smiled
as he raised his glass to General Mineral Water.

Your face he also knew, king of the no-truck back-roads,
driving dazed with an east-west bitumen ball-breaking meta-
stasis. You'd have crushed him. Magnitsky-lawless

Volodya, park your sword. He died with me, here.
The birch-tree pours her sap for the valient gingko.
The *deti* stand to attention, perfect as icicles, whistling

the dream you never had. Red neckties splash
on the padlocks of Matrosskaya Tishina.
*Let there ALways be ME*

is also Caesar's song. But when the *malchik* sings,
listen to him: he's met the gods you worship.
Count him out. Count the many of him there are.


*Notes: **Malchik**: (Russian) young lad.*
***Detski saad**: kindergarten. 'Let there always be*
*the sky, the sun, me' quotes a Soviet children's song,*
***Pust vsegda budet solnce.***
***Volodya** is the diminutive of Vladimir; the latter*
*should be pronounced vlaDImir. The name, **Putin**,*
*is connected to the word for 'road' or 'way.'*
***General Mineral Water**: Nickname of Mikhail Gorbachev.*
***Magnitsky-lawless** refers to the murdered lawyer, Sergei Magnitsky.*
***Deti** — children; **Matrosskaya Tishina**: prison in Moscow.*
*Name literally means 'Seaman's Silence'*

*MCMXLV: For the Poets who Served in World War Two*
*('Never such innocence again', Philip Larkin)*

The conscript poets are leaving us: we still
follow their loose semblance of a formation,
trekking, at its own pace, up an old hill.
Thin, untidy, agreeably masculine,
their outlines, fraying dark against the sun;
unasked, they take their turn at the going-down.

In breaking news unknown
to the children and grandchildren (skim-
fingered at screens) they swallowed bile and dust;
they opened fire. Bundles of pity undone
seemed all they had of youth, but chance returned them
to curious equilibrium: lines that would last.

One cracks a joke, or remembers the words of a tune —
a little sentimental, a little obscene;
verses float past like days, or fish, or the weather,
catching them, still. And over the pages we stain,
as the soldier poets press on, the Muse sighs, "never…
…Never such loss of innocence again."

## Guide to Civilisation

We must begin each other's history, open
The gallery of half-formed pictures, strip
In the wet-skinned changing-room behind the day,
And sit there, baldly shivering. No thought

Of 'who we are', no looks or language-pride
Should drip into these cells of other-learning.
For exercise, embroider enemy flags.
Try out the scariest warriors' chin-lifts, breathe

The gas that wreathes both runners and the dying,
But in the blistered cages which were not
Metaphor, place no candles. Undertake
Responses lighter than an ash-key, swallowed.

The forest is already undertaken.
The strangers un-estranged are old as sunlight.
Physic this transmission; know that knowing
The subway doesn't make all journeys ours.

## *The Grenfell Tower Woman in October*

Do you understand a country of clocks which "go back"?
I keep wishing mine would go back.

Dear tall village, let me again unlock you,
old smell of lifts and stairway, take me, slow, back.

Was it to stretch our citizenship they shouted
*go, stay, this way, no, back?*

Tears are running like us without permission
and not one tear can flow back.

At dawn, we kneel, we wipe, we gulp our Ozone-
Special — the vacuum-cleaner's blow-back.

The kids re-learn their dance-moves. Never tell them
chance was a tooth, won't grow back.

Someone gave them a felt-tip, orange as fear.
I snatch it, scrunch it, throw back

my head and howl *writing names doesn't bring
Samirah, Linda, Jackie, Abdul, Jo back.*

## Cryo-girl's Prayer

not  lying
down     please
not     falling
far from where
my years are folded
in my shoulder
bag     my keys
and doors    coded.

Not broken
down    let me
be contained
like this frozen
self-perfusion
like prosecco
hold me in my
slow    arriving
future-diving
not     dying

days

**Freedom's Twilight**
(open variations on Mandelshtam's "Vote for freedom's twilight")


vote for freedom's twilight girls & boys     and the year's magnificent darkening
          foaming     & heavy falling   everywhere lie
    the filled forest-nets     sun, swing your light up        judge us


vote for the bronze creator boys & girls     you will sweat marble
          to raise him        rough out your cross
      build it carry it   see the state-ship   floundering big time   pity
              our tiny heartbeat


we chained the wings and tricked        the swallows into battle
        the sun blinks itself out     thick nets of twilight smother
                  in twitters, twitches, shimmering
        sunlessness

                                                                    so night-time floats us free


heave girls & boys the wheel the massive helmage              heave until
      horizon creaks   turns     and the land is born
          we are shades        we are unforgetting
      *even in icy fens we paid a thousand  heavens*
              *to keep this earth.*

**The Wooden Swing**
(Two versions, after Mandelshtam's "Tolka chitat...")


1. Upswing


To read only children's stories,
Cultivate little ideas,
And rub away the tears
Of adult categories...

Life? It's a rouble's-worth,
But here's the thing —
I want to sing and sing
My poor, rich, singular earth.

A garden, a child's swing –
I'm flying on the bare
Plank, king of the fir,
through this wild darkening.


2. Downswing


Never to answer emails;
To read kind horoscopes
Only, and let the snails
Chew my envelopes...

What a waste of a good idea,
Childhood was! Light kills
Both snow and clay's career:
Why all these daffodils?

We made a swing for our hopes
On a branch long overgrown.
They've kicked the nettles down.
They jeer from weathered ropes.

## *The Current*

Give me a moment like the one which passed
just now three years ago across your death.

Was it as simple as the exhalation
of any living breath?

Bend its light towards me, warm and strange —
the energy of breath-light. Palpable. Low.
Mirror, window, laptop-screen, work-station,
gatherers all, be space for this respiring
as dust or mist or paring.

There is no need for particles to change,
no different chemistry for 'stay', or 'go'.

### *Exhibits from the Saddest Bedroom*

memory-stick    USB unavailable

columns (dream sequence)     not marble, termite

jaw-mechanism with original skin
soft and unshaven     moved as if to speech

nicknames numbers some still ring

bed-lamp button in cocoon of cobweb

fragile finger trying to get near a closed eye

mattress-stain     small, faded, raspberry-coloured
vagina-diamond

tired white shoes in shoe-hang    long white laces
dripping down    you are allowed to touch them
visitor to try them on to tie them
                                                walk
about in them

## Moon Walks

It was getting late in the year. You had to manage
thirty paces to reach
the last-ditch blueberries.
*Chernika*. Not local fruit, not Russian:
transplanted moonlight, tended, half-forgotten.

You wore your heaviest jacket,
the lumberjack-check, and steered
your stick, determined, hopeful, through the frostless
leaf-crush. A potato-salad carton,
rinsed, threaded on string, swung at your chest.

It's getting late in the year.
I lace my feet in your shoes;
I even wear your carton,
and grope towards black moonlight; let's pretend
it's harvest-bright and waiting, and I'm hungry.

## To Rossiya

I'd meet you in the Summer Garden
where trash and dumped rose-heads foil the glitter
of the wrecked seafacing window. Tsar Petya —
who saw washed sails rise from a Deptford midden –
would still be flying his dead horse.
Linking hands, we'd stroll across Europe,
to bury our kindly chestnut passports
under the rusty patch where Tsvetayeva's rope
sucked out the bitter hook. They'd torch our bodies,
like royal children in the secret room,
because we'd made fun of the national anthem:
"Your **cof**/ fee is/ **red**/ee my **bute**/ eeful/ **lay**dee"

Rossiya, if your face, if the bridge, if senseless lies…

I'm fading into your lensless eyes. *I kiss you.*

***Throat Stones***
('*March has come to the bridge head,*
*Peach boughs and apricot boughs hang*
*over a thousand gates*' Ezra Pound/ Rihaku)

You saved summers of fruit-stones in a carton –
peach, nectarine, plum, your favourite apricot –
not for eventual planting but for eating
or maybe simply cracking
pleasantly in your teeth some far, dry day.

How many miles of rainy skies away,
how many stones if stones
are steps through memory's root-work?
I sniff the flat, dry buds, their flesh-stained pore-holes.

So cattle wander down
to an unfamiliar, brambly ditch, sucked out
by hoof-churned mud. The animals can't
eat or drink. One stumbles, gazes through
dead thorn-mesh.    *Where's the bridge head?*

The musk of apricots is evening mist
rising like a blade that doesn't strike me,
but strokes salt from all my swallowed throat-stones.

*Stepping Stones*

Sometimes, moonlight happens with no moon.
The bath-time goddess dozes;
still, through the opioid vapour, you can see
dark-pale tarmac, chancred camber, grey
grass, and where the hedges blacken. Cease
looking down, you know dirt without looking.
Your rods and cones remember
the semaphores of downtime. Walk
without your torch, or thinking.

If the bright one drops her wet towel on the lane,
you needn't even walk. Lean out and float,
flow with your listlessness. Pretend the lane is vast,
the Champs Elysées or Kremlinskaya Ploschad.
This silver mile is what was called the future.

You've set off, any way, without being asked to.

## Metamorphosis in Nafplio

Once, a schoolgirl-tourist
in a secretive harbour-city,
left the tour-guide, wanting,
as usual, to see for herself.
Bouzouki music was tangling
its cloisonné of strings and air
towards her from an arcade.
One day, she'd discover the words –
*George Seferis, Mikis Theodorakis,*
"Sto Perigiale To Krifo" –
tonight, she knew nothing.
She wandered into the shop,
parted the vines and shadows
of a forest of dresses, chose one,
took it to the changing-room.
It smelled of wild thyme,
and the weave lay coarse and cool
against her skin;
Greek-key pattern mazed the hem.
She blushed like Persephone
and counted out her drachmas
for the careful man who'd never
stared or grinned at her
from behind his counter.
She re-entered the light
and the crowd. She didn't boast
to anyone about her purchase.
When she put it on that evening
she saw she was different:
but it wasn't simply the dress...
It was the finding and wearing
that had formed her into a woman,
and, perhaps, a citizen.

## Anisychia

Death's little wild friend, chattering Anisychia,
already my courier, pushing my trolley from here
to the Peloponnese, proclaiming our personal weather

with aerosol plumes and a data-dump: gut reaction
of ancient machinery, revving the malware, the mischief;
never-quite-lying alarm monger, tacking two S's to 'care',
curating my uninhabitable Chair,

in my tourist bus my kingsize beds my hair – Anisychia!
whipping me over the underworld's hills, hell-circling charioteer.
When Hypnos bangs out the lights, he's my cinematographer.

**Cypresses**
*for Greg Nagy*

Slim shadows, ragged, slightly deformed, not tall,
they were green young athletes once, who, lacking physique
and horse-sense, killed themselves when they jumped on the turn
in the chariot-race. And now they wait for the ferry,
puzzling where between life and death they are,
almost persuaded they've hit the ground running.

## Temple

I watch the old couple, hands linked, like children
on the broad stairway towards the hill-top temple.
The one who limps is talkative, brightly alert.
The other, tall, half-smiling, doesn't quite know where he is.

How desperate I used to be for young love!
I was twenty, the years since school raced hard, I was losing
shamefully, indescribably, some contest
with growing-up. So I got married, still twenty,

and served myself from the urn of mixed delights
and toxins. Now I think, what was the rush?
Old love is best, the real and useful marriage
of minds, administered by impediment.

The old couple steady each other, careful
over the slippery, pearly stone.  I pass them,
single, envious, eager to be the first
to reach the altar-less wreck of the god's temple.

## Seven Stained Glass Panels, with Goats

*This imaginary stained glass window is based on the Trinity Icon.
It portrays God the Father, God the Son and God the Holy Ghost
dining with Sara and Abraham. Lot and Lot's Daughter are also
featured. A chorus of immortal goats narrates 1,2,3, 6 and 7.*

*Panel 1: The Goats consider Abraham*

Only for God-the-Guest
would Abraham fish our dearest kid from the flock.
Guest-Without-Thanks approves this *rum, ram, ruf*
of life well-knifed. Why else
bind all us beasts in the bright
red lace, if shrieks and knife-holes didn't please him?
And the last-second "enough"? Not enough, not enough.
Abraham looks away with his mountain eyes
but hears us goat-mouths mumble – God, Abraham,
Hitler, Dönitz.

*Panel 2: Sara looks at herself*

Skinny, vague, a husk-head,
always behind with the work, the infernal
crying-out-loud of eternal
forceps, fire-tongs, pots, potties, coffins —
*oh, what do I know?* cries Sara.
She wanted a little courtyard
with ceramic blue-birds, lemons,
no kids. She lay in the bath, Diana-shy,
dry-drowning in old-man theology.
At 13, she'd wanted a green Mohican:
she told Abie a girl could be an oak tree,
but the spirit in her ran
thin at his jokes and demons.

21

*I won't sit*, God tells her, *things to do.*
Her wrists seem to be chained. Her hands are wet dough.

*Panel 3: The Goats study the Holy Ghost*

*Just another wasted teenager,*
Sara mutters, *my Abie's always son-struck.*
We edge nearer, heart-shaped nostrils glistening,
lick shins and sniff the spirit.
Holy shit, his bottle-brittle, dried-out, totalled
string of aches! What was the father-sin?
Dad pushed his feathered hollows, yelling *Drink*
*the blood, you bloody girl.*
His own blood's turquoise ink —
proof of artistic talent. Bleat him a song,
but don't kneel, and remember
narcosis is not inspiration,
although he'll twinkle a pun on *pure spirit*
before he keels over.

*Panel 4: That night, old lovers, tented*

D'you think he was annoyed?
*Go to sleep, woman. Who?*
You know. He heard me laughing
*Everyone hears you laughing. Go to sleep.*
He said we'd make a baby.
*He said he made the world*
*in seven days… Shift over.*

D'you think we made a baby?
'How dare you doubt the power of the lord? You laughed!'
he said. I said *I swear I never…*
And he, in his dry, cold voice: *Sara, you did.*
I can't stop blushing now… I laughed, I lied…

*Calm down, there are worse women in Sodom.*

*Panel 5: Lot's daughters*

Mum's salt on the brimstone plain and dad's in pieces,
our past's all raked to potash
and home's a filthy cave, and there's no man for our babies.
Seeds don't grow in a cave.
Look at you, wet and bleeding…
What we're doing ain't natural.

*Shut up and give him a bit more wine,*
*he'll get it together. Bind*
*your thighs round him like I did.*
*He can still pump and sigh.*
*Take him apart with kisses, whisper Our Father*
*which art in thy daughter's heaven,*
*this is as good as it gets.*
*Take a swig yourself and drown*
*your breasts in roses. God,*
*aren't we two angels? Show him he's double lucky.*
*Go for it, sister.*

*Panel 6: Undecorated*

Plain glass, with a message in plainness:
*art is so you  forget*
*that earth is not as beautiful as heaven.*

When you pray, open your eyes, sang Rublev.
The colours kneel, their arms stream towards you
and past you into the brilliant
colourlessness they were and are and will be.

*Art is so you remember,*
*that colour is not flawless,*
*as glass is sometimes flawless,*
God's mind, he's still making it up:

it's a bubble, a goat-hair,
a lichen filament in a database,
a Milky Way Bar in the Milky Way.

*Panel 7: The Goats and the Carpenter*

He loved to watch the old man working, trading,
outside the temple, glass-housed
with potash, oxides, Latin spells and curses,
fattening up the rainbow serpents. Dad
put his hardcore foot down.

The boy dropped his hands — poor acorns, wood too soon.
He understood the contract. Mind-dark wind
splashed the tent with golden leaves and blood-drops,
the serpent burst. *Blow glass!*
He stroked the splinters of his new black beard.
*It's cool to be*
*the table-maker,*
*to bring down the oak tree of Terebinth.*

We keep our horny heads in the branches, munch
the foliage, and hope. Accept our wisdom,
lad, don't trust those lilies;
keep an eye on the rash old knife-twister, fire-builder, absent-
father you call God.
If heaven is art and all its sciences,
you might be the making of him.

## A Christmas Clover Leaf

Trite metaphors of the Christingle!
Sugar an orange for an airbrushed world,
Light the shivering god, the scented candle.
Try metamorphosis: *ingle, christkindl* —
The word explodes, as hope does, in the *kristall*
Of genocide, the flaming darkness, old,
Trite meta-force.
      For each child's Night of Crystal,
Sugar an orange: form a hair-brushed world.

## Cremation Carol

Watered ash-leaves lament: where tree?
   *sing holly berries, sing rose hips*
      *red green green red*
        *seed seen*
      *green red red green*
   *hide cracked lips, hide hollow bellies*
tree where lament leaves ash watered.

Scattered ash-stems wonder: whose tree?
   *sing armistice, sing armaments*
      *known names last names*
        *morphine*
      *dreams seen, lost scenes*
   *hide shadows, tied ropes; cry hopes,*
tree whose wonder stems ash scattered.

*Autistry*

Other people are a well-known difficulty for the autist, that
author of her own otherness, but what isn't often understood
is that the autist feels rarely truly alone: divided into her own
others, the autist is locked into connection with them, and the
associated difficulties of connection. They stare at one another,
judging and striving to impress the judges, minds kept taut
and verbal and busily repetitive by an internet of threatened
disconnections. Self-clones are more real and relentless, but,
admittedly, more tolerable than genetically-other aliens –
shadows of pure mind, which have no separate smell from the
familiar smell of self. When I was a child I gave them colour-names.

***Cat*** (freely, after Baudelaire)

Come to my warm heart, splendid cat, revise
your nails, soften your feet
and let me disappear into those eyes,
agate and jet.

My fingers repeatedly slither
over your head and along your fluent back
till my hand is drunk on your fur
and we *sing the body electric!*

I long for my lover. His stare,
like yours, would be frozen
gun-fire.

From head to toes, his air
of pungent, arrogant black-man
wrecks me with desire.

## Nature in Half Light

as if
one of the birches had walked
and fostered itself upon the
shaggy old grandparent firs

or a lost Greek architect's ghost
said *this must be Athens*

the dawn light reveals
in the trees an inserted column
of calcite paleness;

thin satins fall across paving.

The conversation in the further woods
smoky and frail, is the wavering
onomatopoeia
of *owl*

until the first car shoulders through
the fog to Llanberis.

How well we've made it seem
all an extension of nature.
We put on shells or wings
or stretch up calmly as birches
(our fellow pioneers, rooted in fossil-fuel,
disguised as fountains of lucidity).

The satins flow from us;
our light is our saliva.

Sometimes, I think we may
somehow know enough
(or our guts and mouths may know it) not
to engulf everything.

### The End of Playtime
*i.m. David Rumens*

The childishness of adulthood appals
At times: at others, seems its saving grace.
We often love the person best who calls
The childish, honest, laughing part of us
To life again. We cherished that in you.
You kept our childhoods safe. And now they're crying
In disbelief that Dave could ever do
A cold, relentless, adult thing like dying.

## Life Studies in the 'Seventies
*i.m. Robert Lowell*

When you talked to me in sonnets, time calmed,
horizon slipped to a curious windless shore
where an almost-English voice, mock-casual, swarmed
and twisted like my hair, that henna'd, permed
announcement of the rebel-wife, hot mover
against the tide that sighed, *you're trapped, it's over.*
I hadn't even noticed your confessions:
I rated grit and smoke above "old flames" —
muscular shapes like "B.U. sophomore",
"Colonel Shaw", "*panettone*", "Mattapoisett."
I thought I might add to the gorgeous racket.
Now, what do I care? I've binned my rations.
The new kids hiss "*Hic jacet…* pass it on!"
At least we never get to see our names
on one particular white important jacket.

### Game of Eagles

Two Tsars, appointed by one God,
shake hands, share games, compare the war:
each boasts a mighty phishing-rod.
Twin narcissists, pent by the god
whose love moves stars, they joke and nod –
*Let double-headed eagles roar!*
Two Tsars, app-haunted, (password, *God*),
game on. Fall, shares. Shake, hands. It's war.

### Variations for W S Graham
*on the 100th centenary of his birth*

*I have made myself alone now.*
*Outside the tent endless*
*Drifting hummock crests.*
*Words drifting on words.*
*The real unabstract snow.*
   W S Graham, "Malcolm Mooney's Land"


What everyone thinks, I
suppose, who has time
to form thought-like
shapes during the long
plunge into the crevasse;
many, all their lives,
have traipsed towards it,
equipped but unprepared
ever to hear it hollering back:
*I have made myself alone now.*

The only paradise
is motion, lost
to encampment, both
improvised. Sometimes
the bed must be unfolded
still warm from under us,
torn for another sail;
on the plate, the bleak dog-meat,
outside the tent endless
drifting hummock crests.

Bodies row their own
furrows, wry channels,
other breathers always
just out of earshot.

Now and again the mouth
makes kissing-sounds.
The pack (the pawed god
of the team) will quicken now,
mapping the maps, fresh
words drifting on words.

You know where I'm going
with this. Of course.
It's January, the coarse-
gritted wind of a hundred
Januaries hurtles
from your mound. Yr Wyddfa freckles
with treacherous blackthorn.
High-skilled for the gradient
you're gracing it through
the real unabstract snow.

***At Ladywell Cemetery***
 *i.m. David Jones, and for members of the Mills*
 *and Clark families, also buried there*

In tangled aisles, blank naves,
between the playing-card stones
no prayer but rain engraves,
we found where Private Jones
lies with the shield he loans.

We looked for others, too –
mysterious grandparents,
the little uncle who
continually haunts
sad, octogenarian aunts.

How deep and complicated,
their deaths, their burial.
They learned to count, to read
and write, but wrote too small.
Where are they all?

      ****

From Mametz Wood and Loos,
mouths blaze with rhyme, but when
Demos sifts the chaos,
we watch how class writes men,
in every stripe of pen.

One swanned the lakes of learning,
one peered through a crack.
The languid, Latin-turning,
bard-quoting hack,
the print-boy at his rack

of type, illuminate
gulfs of entitlement.
Then Olwen whispers, *Wait!*
*The hard bench where you learnt*
*your place is innocent.*

*Old wealth? A family-tree?*
*Dinnseanchas sung?*
*There's deeper treachery*
*if, from a blasted lung,*
*dead ayres are wrung,*

*or neurasthenic sighs*
*to a courtier's moon.*
*These are my secret eyes,*
*my dark platoon:*
*Rosenberg, Sassoon,*

*and raw South London's foundling*
*prince of the white caer,*
*who salvaged the shelled kindling,*
*charmed a twelve-tone lyre*
*from the common fire."*

****

We took some pictures, paused
and wandered on,
tourists of the unhoused,
searchers for the unknown,
for chipped wings flown

the vaults and various hollows
of their last battle-field;
names in mossy shallows,
the randomly spilled
breath almost held.

Their parenthetical graves
would barely stain the year,
but he, bright-shielded, weaves
trefoil and sweet-briar,
and binds our mound-kin, here.


**Notes:**
Olwen -  in Welsh myth, a goddess of the underworld.
Dinnseanchas – Irish, a litany of significant
place-names and characters.
Mound-kin – the term is borrowed from
*The Tutelar of the Place,* David Jones, 1961:
    "Remember the mound-kin, the
     kith of the *tarren* gone from
     this mountain because of
     the exorbitance of the Ram…"
The binding of the wild flowers was suggested by
the "Queen of the Woods" passage at the end of *In Parenthesis.*

### The Hazel Nut

(Words and phrases in Middle English spelling are based on Julian of Norwich, *Revelations of Divine Love*)

*E-book and candle,*
*Timber, stars and shade,*
*Moonlight on a thumbnail,*
*And all things made…*

In my palme I held it,
A lytyll singing nest,
Rownde as eny hasyl nott,
The universe compressed.

Torsion of the hairspring!
Who made wealth so small,
So near, we thought it nothing,
So much, we spent it all?

Lunar tourist, weightless
Dreamer of new land,
Finds the single turquoise,
Smaller than his hand.

*Transit-camps, alarm-bells,*
*These I saw and heard —*
*Rattling stones and hollow shells,*
*Sea-rise in the glade,*

And lifeless rock for Lack-Wit,
The king of green things dead,
For lytyll heed we took of it,
The hasyl nott we had.

## To Gwynedd

*'Meseems I see the high and stately mountains*
*Transform themselves to low dejected valleys.'*
*Ye Goatherd Gods', Philip Sidney*


Land of our grandmother, Alys Emily!
Land not entirely unambiguous
in welcome, creasy grin a kind of judgement,
you're so old you're young – wild teenager,
*harddegau gwyllt* —
your slept-in-look eternally morning-after-
the-mountain-rave, petrified evidence
of ruckus, rape and knife-fight. Slumped in riverine
spillage, they who love you
might wake up poets      if they wake up.


Strung out on bright blue lakes
we take the hairpin bends too
Jesus    too
fa    slow down! Volcano madness, this.
They'll kick us soon as look. I hardly see them
for seeing our bones cheese-sandwiched in the landbits
we owned, whose cast-off selves owned all of it
and reasoned, 'Let the Welshman break the stone.'


Payback-seductress, summer Gwynedd fleeces
the fleecy-lined colonists from Chester
and Merseyside and Moscow with
Llanfairpwllgwyngyllgogerychwyrndrobwllllantysiliogogogoch,
with pretty inn-signs, warmish beer, sogged fries.
She drains the thirsty drop-outs from all over,
to her sale of mushroom-magic, yurty glamping,
the rock 'n' roll of waterfall and runoff.
Old music-mouth, old gossip, mocker, peace-

offering your ironic cartoon dragon
to Grendel's fossil claws,
Gwynedd, don't be angry!
Our shiny notes are bankable, at least.
Don't die to us. Let's end our letters only
as Alys Emily Davies, gifted in
the paler dragon's tongue, used to end hers to me,
on the last page of her dainty mountain-ranges,
"Must close for now, dear. Yrs Affectionately…"


(Stanza 3, line 4, the Angelsey place-name translates
 as "St Mary's church in the hollow of the white hazel
near to the fierce whirlpool of St Tysilio of the red cave")

*Briallen*

Notched petals brimstone-pale, your bee-star, orange-gold —
none of the English poets saw, but Clare.
The name sufficed, they thought; and so you disappear.

Take up your Welsh name, primrose, a small downpour
to freshen you, the common, un-lost flower,
sun-wink of sudden waking in your crinkled foliage-fold.

## Sestina Colada

'Write me a poem', says Tina.
'You've got to have some rhyme
To make it keener, meaner
And, hopefully, sublime.'
I say 'I'll have a Piña,
Colada, if there's time.'

To catch and tame and time
The spin of your sestina
Requires a rum-rich Piña.
It lubricates the rhyme.
Old Swinburne was sublime.
I'm minor, but I'm meaner:

Despite the calm demeanour
I'm counting down the time
Till Tina cries, 'Sublime!'
And love is a sestina
Where couplets dare to rhyme
Like Tina with her Piña,

I've watched her strip a piña,
For "Ananas Carmina" —
Culinary terza rima
That drips with summertime
And tastes like the Sistina
Capella looks — sublime.

Ironic word, 'sublime'.
It's worse than a subpoena
For every line. Sestina
Lente. It gets meaner.
Oh, Tina, give me time:
One more, before I rhyme.

Around my chin there's rime.
My snooze was not sublime.
I had a fight with Time
And slept with Agrippina
Who's like a man, but meaner…
'Here, Tina, my sestina –

The rhyme divine as Piña,
Love, a sublime pashmina
For time. 'It's crap', says Tina.

### Chain Reaction: Uranus, Uranium...

The black rock, mantled by silverings,
rings like hammered metal in the mind:
mined with no master plan, planet new to the light
of day, of night,

light up our dark, let us. Channel the untenable
chain-reactions. Actinide. Acridine. Eye-dazzle
dizzying waterscool hot-jacuzzi-white —
and the cloud is bright

though it covers the sun... Undone
atom, your ovum
is not unlike a poem
or any wild run.

# Threnody, with Depleted Uranium

*My love, I loved you well, I kept you well.*
*I kept you as musk in the box and as wire in the reed.*
*I kept you as a silver lamp which lit up this home.*

On the day when our fingers and lips were broken mirrors,
I stayed in the kitchen, though I wanted to see
as they packed you in a long bag. They wheeled you past me.

Then they hid you in a long box of pale oak
and out of the flames they brought me a little salt
in a cardboard tube printed with pastel flowers.

I keep your arms and shoulders in a wardrobe of old sweat-shirts.
Your feet are wrapped around mine as I walk in your shoes.
Your head moves shyly in small photographs.

I will send you into space, to flirt among girlish moons.
I will bury you in a mine as deep as the nights
when I think the words 'never' and 'not ever.'

My hand passes through concrete, and brings out mud and ash
and the intermittent sparks of atomic decay.
I will keep you well, Ouranos, my silver-suited darkness

and live with your death unburied at my core,
as the planet lives with the half-life of a great metal
*that creates deadly hazards when used in anger.*

## Star Tin Ga Cha: Fission Fragments

1.

In nuclear fission atoms are split to release energy
in a nuclear reactor uranium atoms are forced apart
the fission products cause other atoms to split
starting a chain reaction.

2.

clear ion at rest lit or lease
actor ran o for a part
ion rod duct    her atom
splits art in ach! inaction

3.

In-nu cle arfis sio natom
sares plittor e lea seen
ergy inanu cle-ar rea
c'toru rani uma tomsa
ref orc eda part ther e sult
ingfis sion pro ductscau
se oth era toms tos plit
star tin ga cha in react ion

### Message from an Optical Implant

In the tissue sac your eye
made itself, my polymer does fine;
it filters the essential tiny traffic
through to the optic nerve
waving it on, no road-blocks, no arrests.

Call me a whale's dried tear, a broken
coral branch, an omen
from seas stiffened with dunes,
your flightless future.
Call me death, but admit I'm nicely measured
to the miniature sphere, your eyeball, where I shine
with good-cop goodness. German factory *phakos*,
no secret visionary, plain wicked plastic,
I'm ringing in your bluebell winter morning,
your midnight clear, your first
stars this century.

## A Different Vision

And when the bright detail was restored,
all my senses danced, until Ravel's
Kaddish, rinsed with too much sunshine, scalded
the morning with a blinding rain. I saw you
and thought if only I'd been more aware
of all my retinal glitches, darnings, rainbows,
I could have seen more clearly how to love you.
What shall I do with all this finer light?

## Farmers in Empty Fields

Bribe-wheat, whimsy-grain,
  What time should we harvest you?
    *Time is over,* sighs the grass.

Pixie-liquor, lichen-wool,
  What can we use to process you?
    *Stills and looms,* mocks the grass.


Lemma, palea, never still,
  Will your flour amount to bread?
    *For us, for us,* sings the grass.

### Penmon Point, November

The wind flowing across the lens-bright Strait,
knit of slatey lustres with sand-green
opacity, shades with shallows...

Rocks in their dinosaur sorrows
quietly absolve the quarrelling spectra
that spin the wild new blue in their old blue world.

Kyffin Williams
*Sunset Over Penmon*

***Ynys Iago, with Cats***
***(for Sharon and Mark)***

Iago's Island: cars sweep by
   the green strand of the fields all day and most

watches of the night, long airless gasps
   of coming, leaving    leave me

story-done    imperial litter    (kings
   pass like traffic, too).   I run a diner

for smaller beasts & rarely one puts up
   for the night    feigns to love me   murders the blanket

pleading hunger    hotly
   scours my stroking hand    drowns it in tongue.

Iago, Iago, when the isle was grass
   you were the beast-in-residence    remembered

by taller children now    the quarryman's house
was named for you, your long horse-sighs, your shadow, Ynys Iago.

## Swept beyond Penmon: Kyffin Williams in the After-Sea

"One summer evening, not long after I arrived at Pwllfanogl, a friend came to visit me
with his small son aged five. As we stood at the water's edge, with gentle waves breaking at
our feet, the little boy looked up at me:

'What will happen to you here when you die?' he asked with a look of concern on his
face. I knew I had to answer with a confidence I did not possess.

'Oh, it will be wonderful,' I said. 'I shall slip into the sea and be swept away by the
water, and I shall be carried under the bridges and away to Penmon and the open sea. Oh,
yes, it will be rather wonderful.'

As he listened to me the worry seemed to disappear from his face and he ran off to
throw stones into the waters that were to carry me away…"

*A Wider Sky*, Kyffin Williams  (Gomer, 1991, Llandysul)

### 1. Diagnosis

After a glance at my encephalogram,
the doc remarked, "*Young man,
You appear to be abnormal: take up art.*"

Hadn't the bastard any sympathy?
Hadn't he realised to be young and *abnormal*
is to be axed, to stare at your bare, twisted

hands, emptied; wait for the ice-headed nails,
like long mean eyes from the normal soldier's sockets,
to drive into your heel-bones?

Christ himself as he took his bow at Canaan,
thought *I should be the dancing bridegroom, not
some freaky kid-magician with no girlfriend,*

*the Son of God the Son of God Knows What
doing stuff   I don't know how   weird-gifted
because Pa says, and Mama weeps and whispers.*

God alone knows what hit me, why my tears
at the stink of paint blazed into loaves and butter.

One none-too-starry night Vincent vaulted over
the dikes to Kentish Town. *Hé makker, wat wil je drinken?*

He smeared me with his grin of brotherly pain,
wrapped my crooked head in his months-old bandage.

*All painting's tricks, but never be led by tricks.*

That's Welsh, I thought.  I saw my own black sunlight.

### 2. The Farmer Views the Painter

He liked to catch a figure
                         moving

                                            out of the canvas –

                              said it meant the day
      behind the man was realised

He talked of having seizures   see     but it's seizure

of seeing he has       he sees
the back of my head    the mountain behind it   the other

   side of the mountain  how it

steadies the sky
keeps it in place      and us ahead       he sees.

He realised days   not frames. Rocks, headwaters, roars
   of the universe, no close-down.

My dawns sketch smaller    seasons
mix      the high mind hazes.

Give me a face    Kyffin bach
like the sunflower the Dutchman painted.
That man had seizures   too

                Give me my face
                    as I go

   You say the day behind me
      is realised   I say
                    tell the bloody mountain
                        to walk out of the picture, and let the man be.

### 3. Crucifixion

God comes in a dream and stands behind my easel.

*Still painting your nudes*

*like blasted oak-trees, Williams?*

Sir, this
admittedly heavy man

slid from my hands     torn up like fishing boats
in an Atlantic gale
I pitied his simple whiteness, heard the lashed wood
speaking Cymraeg
though felled and sawn and planed and nailed with Latin

Resurrection ought to have eyes like fire-alarm bells
but I couldn't see them here
{ forgive me, I'm not Piero della Francesca }
no lights for my carpenter
as he tries to love the burning

His flesh felt soft to my touch like Patagonia's rocks
damp as the week's wash a settler wife
hangs on the wind     the disloyal     imperial
ever-soldiering wind

Sir   I held him firmly to his branching

**4. *Cross Bar*** (from found texts by
Ieuan ap Hywel Swrdwal and Kyffin Williams)

O trysti Kreist tat werst a krown
er wi dei down, aredi dicht
  tw thank tw thee
    at te rwt-tre.
Dden went awl wi
ddein own, rw licht.
Tw grawnt agri
amen wy mi
ddat ei mae si
Ddi tw mei sicht!

The most successful bird I painted
Was a cock pheasant, not because
I'd rendered beauty
Beautifully:
The beauty was
That I shot it
Painted it
Ate it
Sold it.
Not even Rembrandt
Ever did that.

## 5. *Resurrection Prayers*
*i.m.  KW and YD*

Ocean Iapetus, warm, carboniferous,
born here, lived, burned dry here, raise your foam —
blackthorn over harebells.

Roam in your lichen coats, Ordovician
volcanoes; breed green swords
of seedy sward, from Gwynedd to
Catraeth. Drift, lava-seas,
ash-seas, Snowdonian ossuaries, weather-ghosts.

Glaciers, flow down, like memory-stains
from tombs, to the Menai faultline.

Fast-running ice, he sailed you. Glacial
erratics, stranded, he scaled you: rest

as tuff and till, settle
gradually down with the slowed
cancer and cancer-damage at Rhyd y Groes.

In the Chapel of Rest
lovers' fluvial secrets, land-
locked until now, fold into siltstone and cromlech,

taking the dots of colour, last-thought words or lingering
tactile flits      (a moth hangs up her brown coat
in a small dark hide in the chapelry of Pentir).

Heather and fern and sand-footed seagulls, boldly
stamp the drowned sub-continent;  semaphore Pangea
leaving British waters;  ports, flare open.

You rocks that have eaten fire, play like moonlit
children and the quietest seas. And you
metamorphic ones, be the weather of human faces.

Night-painter, never wake, clasp your knife lightly.
Make us a mountain, a churn of sunlit butter,

for a single hand can blend all lonely tide-stuff,
the blue green ocean-mix of Traeth and Tierra del Fuego,
show latitude long slow routes like drovers' roads —

our lanes just wide enough. Lon Carfan's hedgerows
breathe out      beloved, your last short walk                out to where the Atlantic
leaves for Patagonia and Kamchatka.

*A Toy Divan*
 *(Divan-e-haal-e-atfal-o-naunihal:*
 *the book of the condition or mystical state of the babes and cherubs).*

## Grumpy

before
old age
picks me
apart
why shouldn't I
pick
apart the age?

## Remembering

You were an immigrant.
You found asylum here,
Your English hardly fluent,
Your fashion slightly square.

One smile, and we swapped faces.
I was the migrant. You,
The native, clocked my strangeness,
But smiled and waved me through.

We sailed a halcyon raft;
We lit each other's eyes.
I've learned, alone, adrift,
It's laughter first that dies.

## Poetry Criticism

He makes all the *chef* gestures –
spins to the stove, tips the lids, inhales.
You can almost taste the aroma
(at least, the aroma of his ecstacy).

Then he dishes up
three pieces of unmatched Lego.
*His signature dish*, the reviewers
nod to each other, unfolding
napkins, adding a scrunch of black pepper.

## Nostalgia

Unassuming Democrats
Still rage to turn things round;
Deploring Donald and his brats,
They'd bleed for their lost ground

Of neo-liberal sublime
Where slaves rest from their labours,
And law is innocent of crime
And everyone's good neighbours.

Apocalyptic Britishists,
As well, would spin things round.
In the beer gardens of Penge West,
They blub for their lost ground

And bawl for Empire's bloodless plain –
The wealth, the sport, the order!
They'd be a nation once again
If Sydenham had a border.

## The Civilisation Test

Here's your first question: an essay
on "How to Read a Statue".
(No, not "statute" – *statue*,
As in Michelangelo, yes - or Cecil Rhodes).
Sorry! It's very hard. It would be hard for us, too.
But we are already civilised.
We are allowed to skip it.

**The Cut** (loosely based on Katerina Anghelaki-Rooke's 'The Barber Shop')

After you left my bed I followed you
Into the dirty sunshine of the day
Where you had other business. Yes, I knew
The hopelessness of all I hoped to say.
If you'd gone straight to her front door – and, hell,
I thought you would — I'd have just walked on by:
The barber's, though! Steamy theatrical
Of skulls and musk and naked laughter! I
Slipped in and found a seat (they knew me there).
Your face, rose-red, anointed, naked, shone.
The damp white towel was slicked with fallen hair.
You smiled into the glass. I was undone.

Your stylist, poised behind you, winked at me –
The frump ex-girl-friend, ancient history.

## A Love Poem?

To dream about the dead and about you –
Alive, but dead to me —
My face a window yours stares coldly through,

Clarifies nothing, though the story's true.
It's the old compost-muse, Mnemosyne,
Livens the dead, and, dead to life, dreams you.

The dead are sympathetic. One or two
Open their wobbly arms repentantly,
But I'm a window, now, and you'll walk through

Without a shiver. Don't care if you do.
Don't live in Hotel Heartbreak, now: I'm free
Never to dream of you.

What if we really met? *Gosh, how time flew,*
We'd say, and hesitate, and almost see
The cracks which, less than winds, we vanished through.

No praise I sang before would I review.
Again you'd seem all grace, all poetry...
And though you wished me dead, I'd offer you
Your window, still lit up as you walked through.

### Eva Larkin's Lost Letter to Philip about the Weather
  For James Booth

Well, creature, I don't mind my summers cloudless.
What I must try to rip out of my fur,
over and over, is war. My thunderstorms
are air-raids, tearing roofs off, babies flying —
I always see them flying — and the bomber,
his sewage vengeance. Oh, if you were here
I'd clap my paws, catch doodle-bugs and squash them —
if you were here…
                    You live near trees, get 'high'
on jazz, and 'blue' from pollen and committees.
You sneeze and tease! The poems shine regardless.
Dearest creature, sometimes I'm quite stunned
from all I fear. My jazz is 1940s,
but pleasureless, a curdling sick glissando,
a no-beat shriek. My only peace is 'cloudless' —
that empty sky of youth. I nearly swam there.

## Blackthorn Winter

*The 'blackthorn winter' is the traditional name*
*for the mid-May period when there is still frost at night,*
*but the blackthorn is in flower*

*i.m. Tony Conran*

The sun in the frost-haze,
or half in a bruise
of cloud, makes fine
white porcelain.
*Banquet, banquet,*
the finches sing,
as the black wood spreads
its blossom platter.

And the dead will drink
friendship from jasper,
and bless the tough stars
of night, which are yours,
which are all our fruit.

# A Qasīdah for Aphrodite on Her 77ᵗʰ Birthday

## 1.

Desire gives up on men at a certain age, it's said.
Luckily, I'm a woman, and still see her bubble-cut head
through windows near and curtains far; I sense her
breath, her weight on tissue growing tenser,
milk-heavy…so I bring her this nocturnal
rambler-rose, and swear the blush eternal.

## 2.

Desire, whatever-your-name-is, aisling, bloody cow,
misleader, lead me now
over the melting glaciers of my shame
to rubbly foot-hold. Tell me how we came
to Arctic Lesbos, docking in a fission
of stars. At the beginning of our mission,
we drank the whole galactic universe,
this 'she' I barely saw, in her hieratic blaze,
and I, beside myself
                       suddenly looking down
to find my solid island almost gone.
I slashed and starved to fix that dwindling floe
in damned banality – love for one who doesn't want to know.

## 3.

I chilled, went formal, once I learned my place.
And then she rang me. Breathless, green of face,
I hear the news: her favourite boy has died —
and she invites me to the funeral! Pride-
marcher Desire, don't say we're friends again?
Entranced, enfolded in the pantheon,
I'm like a child between its parents, two
governments, grave Anteros and you,
and shivering like a sacrifice. I'm stuck
with borrowed time for years, a wailing smidgeon of bad luck.

4.
Desire, that's not my only, or my last, report.
You've been a song, a town, a passing thought,
a poem or 2, you've politely acted dead,
and once you drowsed beside him in my darling's bed.
I kissed his dying lips, as now I kiss
all sorts of little things which once were his
and still bear traces of his DNA.
(I ought to dust that lamp-switch. No no no, I can't, today.)
Why does this new bright blood well from the oldest scar?
Doesn't it prove the heartless, brainless, murdering force you are?
I fled, I'm still in flight, feeling despised but knowing
there isn't even that, no feebly glowing
speck of anything as meant as hate.
Desire, why should I summon you so late,
and light the scented candles? It's December,
when families meet to nourish and dismember
each other, claiming sacrament. So join my happy guests,
Desire-Diana! Let your numerous breasts
be moon-tipped waves. My boat still floats: Cythère
is welcoming lifestyle-refugees this year.
The children think we're pissed, and past it. Still
they tease us, *Go for it!*
                Tell me we will.

## *Told You*

We rush in we pour down     we don't say excuse us   you can't
not know it   we're coming     & who we     of course we're the children
you spilled on the world when you     didn't you   loosen we loosen
with laughter     we swirl across   thick across borders & thresholds
windows left licked     we eat plaster & stairways   hector you
up the high wall     past the washing-tanks     deserts, tsunamis
deleting your last-bubble cries     we can see
time's still shining fine   when we sort of half   sort of hear   sort of
some stuff that's beginning far off     and we sing     or sit laughing like babies
full of our lives     and we're hurled   they rush in they pour down
amazed into sand   we know them we know   they're the children
the meaningless children

***Yahrtzeit* Candle**

*In Jewish tradition, the Yahrtzeit candle is lit to commemorate the dead*
*one year after their demise.*

1.
It was the smallest birch-log –
about a hand-span – pulled from
a stack of boughs, fresh-cut.
Perfect, I thought, but when I turned it upright,
found soreness scored
in the moist dark-yellow heartwood,
a single splinter screaming
the chainsaw's slip-up.

I shrouded my dislike (my self-dislike)
and learned mechanics, how a plain white candle
pierced by that needle, finds its
own slight, elegant incline,
and the bark-paper begins
to peel, and yield *smetana*, peanut-butter,
*chorniye khleb*,
snow-stored *vodichka*, the bottle crusted
with frost, a flask of room-warm Irish whiskey.

2.
Fire: I had forgotten
how intricately it lives
with air. I crossed the softly
birch-leaf-puzzled field, carefully stepped
from slate to slate to the threshold;
the flame shuckled, lengthened, shrank
and a gasp of broken sapphire
looked like its last.
My lungs, my skin, felt nothing.
It was all plain air to them.

I have no prayers. I stand
watching the flame, indoors,
watching some nether-whisper
quirking, forking the flame-tip —
things that are deaf and blind and joined; without
knowing, trying, grained
into each other deeper
than gender, unimpressed
with speech, that recent anguish
of cut and splinter.

As birch-trees float themselves
out of an atmosphere
of closing origins,
into all weather, come,
be nothing, anything —
the mottled leaf, the broken
stump, its growth-rings cold,
the latest breath no longer
ours no longer stirring;
come, be anything,
nothing, but never memory.

***To the Sun's Green Flame***
(after 'O Nobilissima Viriditas' by Hildegarde of Bingen)

Oh most resplendent Green, you live in the sun,
rooted in its contained, calm energy;
you are the turning point of space and time.
Cradled by the ministry of your lovers,
your light flowers, and amplifies our earth.
As dawn crosses the sky your slow blush deepens.
You leap, oh sun's green flame.

Spotless, vivid, silken like the noblewoman's dress,
spun from incandescence, shelled
in pearl no nets can reach,
though the navigator sings imaginary numbers,
superlative Green, our virgin love enfolds you.

In the sealed wombs and breast-buds of dark winter
you sleep to rise again. You gleam in wells, preserve
your fire under the snow… and we will be your garden
until the sun folds all our leaves     into eternal shadow.

**Bibliography: Poetry Collections and Pamphlets***
A Strange Girl in Bright Colours (Quartet, 1973)
A Necklace of Mirrors* (Ulsterman Publications, 1978)
Unplayed Music (Secker, 1981)
Scenes from the Gingerbread House* (Bloodaxe 1982)
Star Whisper (Secker, 1983)
Direct Dialing (Chatto, 1985)
New and Selected Poems (Chatto, 1985)
Icons, Waves* (Starwheel Press, 1986)
The Greening of the Snow Beach (Bloodaxe, 1988)
From Berlin to Heaven (Chatto, 1989)
Thinking of Skins: New and Selected Poems (Bloodaxe 1993)
Best China Sky (Bloodaxe 1995)
Holding Pattern (Blackstaff, 1998)
Coming Home* (bi-lingual text with Jerzy Jarniewicz, Book Art Museum, Lodz)
The Miracle Diet (with illustrations by Viv Quillin, Bloodaxe, 1999)
Hex (Bloodaxe 2002)
Poems, 1968-2004 (Bloodaxe 2004)
Blind Spots (Seren, 2008)
De Chirico's Threads (Seren, 2014)
Animal People (Seren, 2016)
Perhaps Bag: Poems (Sheep Meadow Press, 2017)

*As Editor*
*Making for the Open* (Chatto 1987)
*New Women Poets* (Bloodaxe, 1991)
*Two Women Dancing: Selected Poems by Elizabeth* Bartlett (Bloodaxe, 1994)
(With Ian Gregson) *Old City, New Rumours* (Five Leaves Press, 2011)

**Literary Criticism**

*Self into Song* (Bloodaxe-Newcastle Poetry Lectures, Bloodaxe, 2007)

**Prose Fiction**
*Plato Park (Chatto,* 1987, Flamingo, 1988)

**Carol Rumens** was born in Forest Hill, South London, in December 1944. She apparently spent her first two weeks of life in an underground air-raid shelter, in the company of another new-born baby -- male, and, no doubt, an important early influence. She went on to enjoy further illumination from many years of Catholic schooling. She studied philosophy for a time at London University, and then chose marriage, children and the famous University of Life as the most useful training grounds for a poetry-hopeful.

She has published twenty-one collections of poetry, a figure which includes pamphlets and selected editions containing new work. Among her various awards are the Alice Hunt Bartlett Prize for her second collection, *Unplayed Music* (shared with Thomas McCarthy), a Cholmondeley Award, and the Prudence Farmer Prize. *Star Whisper* (1983) was shortlisted for the Dylan Thomas Award and *Holding Pattern* (1998) for a Belfast City Arts Award. *Perhaps Bag: Poems* (New York, Sheep Meadow Press, 2017), containing 21 new poems, was nominated by the Washington Independent Review of Books as the Best Collected Poems of 2017. http://www.washingtonindependentreviewofbooks.com/index.php/features/july-2017-exemplars-poetry-reviews-by-grace-cavalieri
Her pamphlet from the Emma Press, *Bezdelki: Small Things,* with illustrations by Emma Wright, received the Michael Marks Award for Best Poetry Pamphlet published in the UK in 2018.

Carol Rumens has held various University Writing Residencies, including those of Poet in Residence at Queen's University, Belfast, Northern Arts Fellow at Newcastle and Durham, and British Council Writer in Residence at the University of Stockholm (1999). Three poetry lectures delivered at Newcastle University were published as *Self into Song* by Bloodaxe in 2007. She currently teaches Creative Writing at the University of Wales, Bangor, and finds herself to be one of a dying species, the Professor of Creative Writing elevated to that position merely on the grounds of having published original creative writing. However, she is proud to have a gained in 2006 from a Certificate in Teaching in Higher Education, and she takes enormous pleasure from working with student poets, learning from them at least as frequently as teaching them.

In 2001, she obtained a Distinction in the Postgraduate Diploma in Writing for the Stage. Her plays have since been produced in London, Manchester and Newcastle. She has also published a novel, *Plato Park* (Chatto/ Flamingo,1987/88) and has had a number of short stories broadcast on BBC radio. Her work has appeared in numerous poetry anthologies, and she has edited several; most recently, in collaboration with Ian Gregson, *Old City, New Rumours*, a selection of work by contemporary poets associated with the University of Hull (Five Leaves Press, 2011). She also edited Elizabeth Bartlett's *Selected Poems: Two Women Dancing*, Bloodaxe, 1996) and Maurice Rutherford's *And Saturday is Christmas: Collected Poems* (Shoestring, 2011). Her translations from the Russian (with her late partner Yuri Drobyshev) are included in several collections, including *After Pushkin* (Carcanet, 2001) and *Selected Poems by Yevgeny Rein* (Bloodaxe, 2002). Russian, Romanian, Polish, French, German and Chinese translations of her own work have also been published.

Her work-in-slow-progress includes a new novel, new poems, and a selection for Carcanet Press of her 'Poem of the Week' commentaries (Guardian Books Online) to be entitled *Smart Devices*.